Simple Machines at Work

by Mary Katherine Tate

PEARSON

Scott Foresman

Editorial Offices: Glenview, Illinois • Parsippany, New Jersey • New York, New York
Sales Offices: Needham, Massachusetts • Duluth, Georgia • Glenview, Illinois
Coppell, Texas • Ontario, California • Mesa, Arizona

Photographs

Every effort has been made to secure permission and provide appropriate credit for photographic material. The publisher deeply regrets any omission and pledges to correct errors called to its attention in subsequent editions.

Unless otherwise acknowledged, all photographs are the property of Pearson Education, Inc.

Photo locators denoted as follows: Top (T), Center (C), Bottom (B), Left (L), Right (R), Background (Bkgd)

1 Brad Wynnyk/Fotolia; **6** (T) image100/Getty Images; **7** Brad Wynnyk/Fotolia; **10** Vstock/Alamy Images; **12** DK Images.

ISBN: 0-328-13224-1

When someone says the word *machine,* do you think of a slide or a jar lid? These objects really are machines. They are called simple machines. Simple machines help you do work with less force.

3

There are six kinds of simple machines. Have you ever seen any of these machines before?

To understand how simple machines work, you need to know about force. Force makes things move. You use force when you push against something or pull something.

Look at the pictures. In one, a boy is lifting a heavy box. In the other, a boy is using a ramp. It takes less force to slide the box up the ramp than to lift it up.

A ramp is a kind of simple machine called an inclined plane.

Inclined planes make it easier to move things up or down.

The road in this picture is an inclined plane. The slide on your playground is also an inclined plane.

inclined plane

wedge

A wedge is another kind of simple machine.

An ax is a kind of wedge. It goes into the wood and splits it apart.

A screw is also a simple machine. The lid of a jar and the bottom of a light bulb are both kinds of screws.

Screws make it easier to put things together. Think about the lid on a jar. As you turn the lid, it screws down onto the jar, closing it tightly.

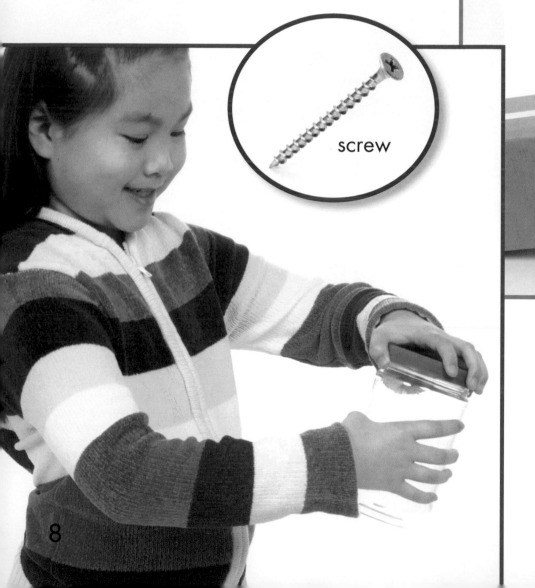

screw

lever

In the pictures above, you see levers. A lever is a simple machine for pushing things up. When you push down on one end of the lever, the other end goes up.

Did you know that a seesaw is also a lever?

pulley

A pulley is a simple machine used for lifting things.

When you pull on one end of a pulley's rope or chain, whatever is on the other end goes up.

The child in the picture above is using a pulley to hoist the flag.

The last simple machine is a wheel and axle. The axle is a kind of rod, or bar, that goes through the wheel. Together, they turn and help things move.

Cars, bikes, and wagons all use wheels and axles.

wheel and axle

Simple machines make it easier to do work. They let you move an object with less force.

People have used simple machines since long ago. We still use them today. All kinds of workers are glad to have simple machines.